C000242485

Marilyn Monroe

Pocket BIOGRAPHIES

Marilyn Monroe

SHERIDAN MORLEY
AND
RUTH LEON

SUTTON PUBLISHING

First published in 1997 by
Sutton Publishing Limited · Phoenix Mill
Thrupp · Stroud · Gloucestershire · GL5 2BU

British Library Cataloguing in Publication Data

A catalogue record for this book is available from the British
Library

ISBN 0-7509-1510-2

Typeset in 13/18 pt Perpetua.
Typesetting and origination by
Sutton Publishing Limited.
Printed in Great Britain by
The Guernsey Press Company Limited,
Guernsey, Channel Islands.

CONTENTS

ACKNOWLEDGEMENTS

The authors would like to express their gratitude to the editors and proprietors and columnists of many newspapers and magazines consulted, some alas long defunct, but others including the *New York Times*, *New York Post*, *Saturday Review*, *Herald Tribune*, *Life* and *Time*. They have also of course consulted many of the five hundred or so books which contain references to Marilyn's life or work, and are especially grateful to the memoirs of Arthur Miller, Lauren Bacall, Norman Mailer, Truman Capote, Yves Montand, Billy Wilder, Simone Signoret, John Huston and the collected film reviews of Pauline Kael. All direct quotations are of course acknowledged in the body of the text.

CHRONOLOGY

1 June 1926	Norma Jeane Mortenson born in Los Angeles
Jan. 1934	Mother institutionalized
13 Sept. 1935	Norma Jeane begins a two-year stay in a Los Angeles orphanage
19 June 1942	Marries Jim Dougherty
1946	Changes her name to Marilyn Monroe
26 Aug. 1946	Contracted to Twentieth Century Fox
13 Sept. 1946	Divorces Jim Dougherty
1947	Her first film appearance in *Scudda Hoo! Scudda Hay!* is cut out in the editing room; *Dangerous Years*
Aug. 1947	Her contract with Twentieth Century Fox is cancelled
1948	Contracted to Columbia Pictures, March to September; Ana Lower dies in the summer; *Ladies of the Chorus*
1949	Appears in *Love Happy* for less than a minute with Groucho Marx
1950	*A Ticket to Tomahawk*, *The Asphalt Jungle*, *The Fireball*, *All About Eve*, *Right Cross*
Dec. 1950	Signs a seven-year contract with Twentieth Century Fox; meets Arthur Miller for the first time

Chronology

1951	*Hometown Story, As Young As You Feel, Love Nest, Let's Make It Legal*
1952	*Clash by Night, We're Not Married, Don't Bother to Knock, Monkey Business, O'Henry's Full House*
1953	*Niagara*; co-stars with Jane Russell in *Gentlemen Prefer Blondes; How to Marry a Millionaire* with Betty Grable and Lauren Bacall
1954	*River of No Return; There's No Business Like Show Business*
14 Jan. 1954	Marries Joe DiMaggio
4 Oct. 1954	Divorces Joe DiMaggio
1955	*The Seven Year Itch*; moves to New York and meets Arthur Miller again
7 Jan. 1955	Forms film company, Marilyn Monroe Productions
25 Feb. 1956	Returns to Hollywood to make *Bus Stop*
1 July 1956	Marries Arthur Miller
13 July 1956	Goes with Miller to London
1957	*The Prince and the Showgirl* with Laurence Olivier
7 July 1958	Returns to Los Angeles to make *Some Like It Hot* with Tony Curtis and Jack Lemmon, her first film in the USA for two years
1959	Affair with Yves Montand during the filming of *Let's Make Love*; collapse of marriage to Miller

Chronology

Aug. 1960	Hospitalized during filming of *The Misfits* for drug abuse
20 Jan. 1961	Divorces Arthur Miller
Feb. 1962	On a trip to Mexico meets José Bolanos
19 May 1962	Sings 'Happy Birthday' to J.F. Kennedy in Madison Square Garden, New York
June 1962	The filming of *Something's Got to Give* is suspended
4 Aug. 1962	Found dead in her bed

ONE

NORMA JEANE

I can see your career rising in the East like the sun.

George Sanders

She was born Norma Jeane Baker (although her birth certificate reads Norma Jeane Mortenson) in Los Angeles on 1 June 1926, the illegitimate daughter of Stanley Gifford, a salesman who wanted nothing to do with his mistress's child, and Gladys Mortenson, married for the second time though not to him, her first husband having taken their three children to live in Kentucky. She died Marilyn Monroe on 4 August 1962, having just turned thirty-six, not the greatest actress or singer in the history of motion pictures but certainly its greatest star. If, for the first half of this century, it was Garbo who captured the hearts and minds of film-goers worldwide, for the second half, and long after her death, it has been Marilyn.

Like Judy Garland and Jean Harlow and Elizabeth

Taylor, Marilyn's private life was very often vastly more eventful and tragic than anything she ever did on screen, but uniquely it was Marilyn who plugged herself into the national consciousness and later the national conscience, so that when she died, in the decade that also saw the sudden death of the two Kennedy brothers with whom she was intimately involved and of Martin Luther King, whom she much admired, it seemed not to be the death of just another actress but the tragedy of America itself, somehow always killing the people it most loved.

From the very beginning, her life had all the qualities of a penny-dreadful. Because her father was nowhere to be found and her mother's endless stays in mental institutions meant that she was considered by the local authorities to be an unfit parent, Norma Jeane was brought up in a series of orphanages and foster homes:

> As I grew older, I knew I was different from other children because there were no kisses or promises in my life. I often felt lonely and wanted to die. I would try to cheer myself up with daydreams but I never dreamed of anyone loving me as I saw other children being loved. That was just too big a stretch for my imagination and I never thought I would ever manage

to have people look at me or say my name. I was never used to being happy, so that was never something I ever took for granted but all around me I saw children brought up to be successful, happy and punctual; I could never manage any of that.

There was to be a little luck on her side. When she was eleven, one of her foster families, perhaps unable to cope with the daily demands of a sulky, pre-pubescent misfit, sent her day after day out to the movies, and it was there that she acquired the only education she ever really had until her marriage to Arthur Miller.

Although precise details have often been hard to establish even for her hundreds of biographers, it does seem more than likely that Norma Jeane was an abused child. Although in later life her imagination was often stronger than her memory of the years she was now understandably trying to block from her consciousness, she claimed that she was consistently raped from the age of eight by orphanage staff and foster fathers, and all the evidence seems to point to some truth in those claims. She had been taken in by Grace McKee, her mother's best friend, who was her legal guardian and had promised to take care of her until her mother came out of hospital. But when the weeks dragged into months, 'Aunt' Grace remarried. (Grace McKee became Grace Goddard on her remarriage to Erwin 'Doc' Goddard.) Marilyn's description of what happened then is stark and graphic:

> She drove and drove for a long time without saying where she was taking me. We finally arrived at a three-storey red-brick building. The sign said LOS ANGELES ORPHANS HOME. Emptiness came over me; my heart began beating fast, then faster. I broke out in a cold sweat. I began to panic. I cried. I couldn't catch my breath. 'Please don't let me stay here. I'm not an orphan – my mother's not dead. It's just that she's sick in the hospital and can't take care of me. Please don't make me stay here.' She had to drag me inside.

It was September 1935, Norma Jeane was nine years old and she would stay in that institution until she was eleven. Aunt Grace finally retrieved her, not to return to her home but to live with an aunt, Edith Ana Atchinson Lower, a 62-year-old spinster who gave the severely traumatized child whatever little confidence and self-esteem she carried with her to Hollywood: 'This woman became the biggest influence on my life. She became my Aunt Ana and the love I have today for the simple and beautiful things in life are because of her teachings.' Aunt Ana was very poor and Norma Jeane often had to help her look for bargains to eke out her inadequate food budget. And, 'I thought to myself, are we always going to be poor, standing on stale-bread lines?'

Nobody seems to have wanted her except a 21-year-old aircraft mechanic called Jim Dougherty who, only a couple of weeks after her sixteenth birthday, became her first husband on 19 June 1942. Aunt Grace engineered the marriage, seeking to end her responsibility for the young girl whose mature body was making her too much of a handful. Norma Jeane was happy enough to fall in with her wishes. Jim was the boy next door and at least he was kind to her: 'That first marriage was really just a kind of teenage friendship with sexual privileges. We hardly spoke to each other, and when we did we realised that we had nothing at all in common.' Within months of their marriage Jim was sent abroad on wartime service and Norma Jeane, alone again and deeply depressed, made the first of her many suicide attempts.

When this failed to work, and realizing that Jim was not presently able to support her, she went to work at a munitions factory, where she was photographed in an eye-catchingly tight sweater. Some of these early pictures turned up in pre-*Playboy* sex magazines with names like *Swank* and *Peek*, and well before her nineteenth birthday she joined the Blue Book Model Agency, who were impressed by her vital statistics – Marilyn herself once said that she wished the epitaph on her gravestone to read 'Here lies Marilyn Monroe, 38-23-36' – and on signing her, insisted on shortening and bleaching her mousy hair to its lifelong blondeness. Alone and beginning for the first time to understand that what she had was desirable to a wide range of men, Norma Jeane rather enjoyed her war.

At Christmas 1945, Jim returned to find his bride now determined on a career as a professional model and gave her a bleak choice – no more sweater-girl photographs (and by implication no more casual 'friends') or no more marriage. Unhesitatingly, Norma Jeane opted for the career.

Dougherty had been the most complaisant of husbands; but when he returned from the war to find her already nude on eight million calendars, enough was enough. He had married Norma Jeane and was about to divorce a nascent Marilyn Monroe, an altogether different woman whom he was never to see again. In her search for identity, one which had haunted all of her childhood, Marilyn had now rejected the role of loyal young wife in the hope of something better just over the hills at Culver City.

Even when I was just starting out as a cover girl, I knew that was really not how I intended to finish up. I told myself a million times that I was an actress because that seemed to me something golden and beautiful – not just an art, but a game you played that enabled you to step out of your own loneliness and unhappiness into worlds so bright they made your heart leap just to think of them. I never knew anything about acting; I took no lessons, read no books, went to no auditions. I never even talked about it because I was ashamed to tell the very few people I knew of what I was dreaming, but from the very beginning I knew I had a talent for observation and that I tried to put to good use.

By now her mother was on a brief release from the Norwalk State Hospital for Mental Diseases, and

in the summer of 1946 she and her daughter spent
the only time of their lives together. But all too soon
her mental state forced her back into the asylum, and
although no fewer than six of Marilyn's countless
foster mothers had turned up to celebrate her brief
Dougherty marriage, the divorce meant that she was
once again on her own. Predictably it was Howard
Hughes, having already expressed his passion for Jane
Russell, who first noticed Norma Jeane as another
sweater-girl with movie potential and summoned her
to RKO for a screen test early in 1946. Her pin-up
fame had spread fast and wide, as at least three
photographers were touting photographs of Norma
Jeane, some entirely nude, around the raunchier
magazines and by the time she had Hughes interested
she was already testing at Twentieth Century Fox,
who duly signed her for three years at a salary of $75
a week, which doubled to $150 after six months. The
distinguished actor and later BBC radio star Ben Lyon
was the director of her screen test and it was he who
suggested a change of name:

When I went home with the contract and told my
Aunt Grace that my new name was Marilyn, she
suggested my mother's maiden name, Monroe, to go

with it. From that day on I had to get used to my new name — I had to remember who I was. Most important, I had to learn to spell it: what if someday I was asked for an autograph and I signed it Jeane?

Her confusion about her own name was understandable. She had been born Norma Jeane (with an e) Mortenson but baptized — by the famous evangelist Aimee Semple McPherson — as Norma Jeane (with an e) Baker. At school she had become Norma Baker and as a model she often called herself Jean (without an e) Norman, while her first marriage certificate reads Norma Jeane (with an e) Mortenson which became Norma Jeane (with an e) Dougherty. At one time she considered a completely different identity but a brief flirtation with 'Carol Lind' was dropped in favour of 'Marilyn Monroe' and immortality.

Precisely what she was supposed to do for her $75 a week was never made entirely clear, but certainly the job description was taken to include the sexual servicing of any studio executive or important out-of-town distributor who took a fancy to her obvious charms. 'Now there's a broad with a future behind her', commented the actress Constance Bennett, as the newly named Marilyn Monroe wiggled her way through the studio canteen and it was already clear that she was developing what Laurence Olivier was later to describe as 'a remarkable ability to suggest naughtiness and innocence at the same time'.

Early in 1947 she did get a walk-on role (cut in the editing room) in a curiously terrible picture called *Scudda Hoo! Scudda Hay!*, all about a farmer's son abandoning his girl for his mule. Indeed, even the most devoted Marilyn groupies have only managed to find her in one silent long-shot here, sitting in a boat at considerable distance from the camera. Although Marilyn was now sleeping with the studio boss, Joseph Schenck, he certainly couldn't be said to have done her much, if any, professional or financial good. As Marilyn said: 'To be blunt, I was never kept by any of my studio lovers, I always kept myself and took a kind of pride in the fact that I was on my own.' But at least she now knew that she wanted to be an actress, and she took full advantage of drama and singing and dancing classes the studio was willing to provide.

She had also acquired a tangential kind of fame thanks to her pin-up work. For $50 she had posed naked for a calendar, lying on a red velvet curtain:

'Sure I posed,' she said later, 'I needed the money.' Already she was becoming acquainted with controversy. The US Post Office refused to allow her nude calendar through the mail, and it was to be another decade before Hugh Hefner used it to launch the first and best-selling issue of *Playboy* magazine. She had already been elected Miss Flamethrower by GIs still serving abroad. Another group of soldiers, equally impressed by her photographs, voted her The Girl Most Likely to Thaw Alaska, while the Seventh Division Medical Corps voted her The Girl They Would Most Like to Examine. But you can't buy groceries with titles.

Fox hastily dropped her at the next option renewal opportunity, despite the fact that she sang a couple of numbers impressively enough to win her a first notice from *Variety*: 'Miss Monroe is a pretty newcomer with a pleasing voice and style – she shows considerable promise.'

Freelance now, like hundreds of Hollywood hopefuls, she had an unremarkable role in *Dangerous Years* (1947). Broke, except for occasional modelling jobs, Marilyn often had to choose between food and acting lessons now that Fox was not paying for her education: 'What would make me an actress, acting lessons or hamburgers?' Six months later, that particular problem was solved when she was picked up by Columbia, whose drama coach, Natasha Lytess, was a kind of Svengali in that she not only instilled in Marilyn the basics of acting technique and etiquette but also taught her about reading and music.

Marilyn's first Columbia project was *Ladies of the Chorus* (1948), which gave her a featured role but did badly at the box office. *Love Happy* (1949), which was next, gave her the chance to make a fleeting impression on audiences as the girl who complains, to Groucho Marx of all people, that men seemed to be following her. 'It's amazing', a usually grudging Marx remarked after working with her. 'She's Mae West, Theda Bara and Bo Peep all rolled into one.' Marilyn herself was thrilled with the impact of a single scene that had lasted less than a minute of screen time:

What then happened to me, because of sixty seconds with Groucho Marx, was the kind of thing that could only happen in Hollywood. I was sent on a luxurious six week tour of the country where for the very first time I learned what it must be like to be a big movie star – press interviews in all the local papers wherever I went, television and radio shows and suddenly people seemed to want me.

Everywhere, except in actual movies. When she returned to Hollywood it was again to a dispiriting round of failed auditions, calendar poses, and acting classes which seemed to be going nowhere. Her mother, Gladys, on a short spell out of hospital, remarried and Marilyn never saw her again, although from time to time, when she could afford it, she sent her money.

By the end of the year Columbia too had dropped her and her career seemed to be stalled. Early in 1950 she did get to sing part of one number with Dan Dailey in a disastrous musical western called *A Ticket to Tomahawk*. This again proved to be a false start, but a few weeks later her luck finally turned. By now, she was sleeping with Johnny Hyde, one of the most influential agents in the country. He was fifty-three, thirty years older than Marilyn, and very rich. He also knew that he had barely a year to live because of a weak heart, but decided to devote all his remaining energies to getting Marilyn's career properly launched. She also made friends with Sidney Skolsky, a press agent, who used to talk her up to the studio executives who were his clients and tip her off to the possibility of roles which might suit her.

Hyde had her nose straightened and her jaw softened, and then got her an audition for the director John Huston, still red-hot from *The Treasure of the Sierra Madre*, who gave her a part in *The Asphalt Jungle* (1950), a small but showy role as the young mistress of a gangster played by Louis Calhern. The career which effectively started with Huston was also to end with him, as only eleven years later they made her last completed film, *The Misfits*; for this first encounter his running gag was to have her described as 'Calhern's niece', the word 'mistress' being still taboo. In what was to become recognized as one of the great crime-and-punishment thrillers of all time, we first encounter Marilyn sprawled seductively across Calhern's lap and it was this immediate identification that was to make the first real impact. Already, with first Groucho and now Calhern, she was carving out a sexual image as the young dumb blonde paramour of rich elderly roués. And although her reviews were still minimal ('There's a beautiful blonde, name of Marilyn Monroe, who plays Calhern's girl and makes the most of her footage') at least around the still-small Hollywood community she was becoming familiar on screen and off as an available 'cutie'.

A year or two earlier she might have been the natural successor to Betty Grable, but with the coming of the 1950s a new kind of puritanism had overtaken Hollywood in the midst of its McCarthyite neuroses, and instead of being the wholesome GI pin-up she was inevitably typecast as the Bad Girl from the wrong side of the tracks.

HOLLYWOOD

If she'd been dumber, she'd have been happier.

Shelley Winters

Marilyn Monroe's fifth film confirmed her reputation as a down-market dumb blonde but in very much more stylish surroundings. Joseph L. Mankiewicz's *All About Eve* (1950) was one of the best backstage movies ever made, and the story of Margo Channing (Bette Davis) and her lethal understudy Eve Harrington (Anne Baxter) is perhaps most famous now for Davis telling her guests to buckle their seatbelts in expectation of a bumpy night. But there were some other great moments, not least one in which drama critic Addison DeWitt (George Sanders) is introducing Marilyn, now no longer 'niece' but 'protégée', to a glamorous Broadway first-night party. 'This', he says, 'is Miss Caswell, a graduate of the Copacabana Academy of Acting.' So now, still only on the verge of her twenty-fifth birthday, Marilyn herself had graduated from nude calendar girl, model, movie extra and part-time tart, to feature player of considerable resources. Her billing, of course, remained almost non-existent until the films were re-released at the end of the '50s, with Marilyn's name having now crept above the title.

But all through her amazingly brief career — barely fifteen years from first to last movie — something about Marilyn's remarkable combination of vulnerability and sexuality made it very easy for her to attract a whole succession of willing teachers, advisors, patrons and gurus, many of whom had their own interests at heart but all of whom contributed to the making of the Monroe legend. The curious thing about this legend, however, was its period quality. Her generation was the last of the old Hollywood superstars, but nearly all the others, from Marlon Brando and James Dean to Audrey Hepburn and Elizabeth Taylor, were definably of their postwar time, while Marilyn alone was a throwback to Clara Bow, Jean Harlow, and even Mae West. She was trading in a currency that was already in real danger of devaluation. And she was always astute enough to know her own severe limitations. Subject to frequent panics and a fatal lack of self-esteem, even at the very height of her fame she was bright enough to know that what she had to sell was at best transitory. Her native intelligence told her that if she didn't escape from the poverty and ignorance of her childhood she would never be happy. She escaped from poverty, but her obsession with self-education was a battle she fought until she died. This self-realization haunted her throughout her life. As Shelley Winters, her sometime flatmate, remarked, 'If she'd been dumber, she'd have been happier'. Only Judy Garland was as much trouble to her studios as Monroe was soon to become, but whereas even Garland had come from the professional background of vaudeville, there was nothing in Marilyn's past to prop her up in the bad times. While everyone told her what to be, nobody ever really bothered to listen to what she wanted.

Nor was her career in any way helped by the death of her mentor Johnny Hyde, although his dying gift to her was a seven-year contract with Twentieth Century Fox, the same studio that had first taken her up and then dropped her. Even now, it was not at all sure what to do with the good-time girl who had suddenly shown in two movies (*The Asphalt Jungle* and *All About Eve*) that she could be taken seriously as an actress – George Sanders, her lover in *All About Eve*, noted that she was certainly going to become a star simply because she so desperately needed to do so.

But not yet. After months of indecision, Fox began lending her out to other studios for a succession of B-to-Z movies which threatened, over the next three years, to sabotage all the good that Huston and Mankiewicz had begun to do for her career. The first of these was *The Fireball* (1950), in which she played the girlfriend of roller-skating speedway champion Mickey Rooney. That same year she also played a brief nightclub scene with Dick Powell in *Right Cross* (1950). Next came the newspaper girl in *Hometown Story*, a glamorous secretary in *As Young as You Feel*, a writer's girlfriend in *Love Nest*, and a dangerous gold-digging blonde, yet again, in *Let's Make It Legal* (all 1951).

It wasn't until her thirteenth movie, *Clash by Night* (1952), that she finally landed a key role in a critical and commercial success. This was the Fritz Lang screen treatment of the classic Clifford Odets play, starring Barbara Stanwyck, Robert Ryan and

Paul Douglas. Marilyn played the secondary role of the cannery worker, Peggy, and it earned her her first serious review from the *New York Post*:

> Marilyn Monroe, the new blonde bombshell of Hollywood and a gorgeous example of bathing-beauty art, is a real threat to the season's other screen blondes. This girl has a refreshing exuberance and an abundance of high spirits. When crisis comes along she is also a forceful actress who has definitely stamped herself as a gifted new star, at last worthy of all her studio publicity.

In fact, all the studio was doing on her behalf was mailing out millions of cheesecake stills (publicity shots) but what was now apparent was that she was very good on promotional tours and even had a sharp native wit. Asked by one reporter over the telephone if she had anything on, Marilyn replied, 'Yes, the radio'.

But even now, her masters at Fox were still having tremendous difficulty matching her new-found fame to scripts that might display her to advantage, and they still weren't prepared to develop one for her. As a result, she next found herself in an amazingly all-star cast (Ginger Rogers,

Eve Arden, Paul Douglas, Mitzi Gaynor and Zsa Zsa
Gabor, all except Ginger billed below her) in an
omnibus comedy called *We're Not Married* (1952),
about which the best thing was a review by Otis
Guernsey in the *Herald Tribune*, which remarked
that: 'Miss Monroe looks as though she has been
carved out of a cake by Michelangelo.'

Intriguingly, it was the English director Roy Ward
Baker, on a brief Hollywood assignment, who now
gave Marilyn her first starring role in a serious
drama, *Don't Bother to Knock* (1952). He cast the
hitherto dizzy and sexy blonde as a psychotic
babysitter with a background of mental instability
much like that of her own mother. In a less than
wonderful script the general feeling was that of
Bosley Crowther in the *New York Times*:

Fox have finally thrown Miss Monroe into deep
dramatic waters, and while she doesn't really sink or
swim, you could say that she floats and with that
figure what could possibly be better? She emerges as
a still-sexy dame but now with good dramatic
promise.

At last, Marilyn was delivering on her contract.
Variety, the showbiz newspaper, that year (1952)

noted that her salary 'has gone up faster in the last twelve months than the cost of living', and it was reckoned that her name on a poster was now worth about half a million dollars to any movie which, as Fox were still only paying her $1,000 a week, had, for them at least, to be a good deal. And yet they were still uncertain whether to play her for comedy or melodrama. After the psychotic babysitter, they put her straight into a Cary Grant–Ginger Rogers farce, *Monkey Business* (1952), which was somewhat apologetically lifted from Grant's earlier triumph in *Bringing Up Baby*. Grant was later to say:

> I had no idea that Marilyn would become a big star; if she had something different from any other actress it certainly was not apparent at this time. She seemed very shy and quiet and there was something terribly sad about her. She seemed very lonely: she would come to the set early, go into her dressing room and read and read and read until we called her. Studio workers were always whistling and shouting at her which I think she found very embarrassing; people don't realize just how distressing this can be for a girl. Marilyn was a victim of the Hollywood system; it's very difficult being chased around by the press all the time and they would simply never leave her alone.

This loneliness, noticed by even casual acquaintances, led to her seeking companionship in many less than salubrious transitory relationships. Studio executives still expected their *droit de seigneur* and she had very few friends. One was another emerging sex-object and star, Shelley Winters. Their similar career paths gave Shelley, by far the more stable of the two, a deeper understanding of her beautiful flatmate:

> As Cary Grant says of Marilyn in *Monkey Business*, she was still half-child, 'but not the half that showed'. She was in fact a very peculiar mixture of shyness and uncertainty and star allure and she certainly knew her impact on men even it she was never sure quite what to do about it.

Others were less fond of the new girl on the block; Joan Crawford went so far as to tell the film magazine *Photoplay* that Marilyn represented everything that had gone wrong with modern Hollywood.

But suddenly it looked as though Marilyn's perpetual search for someone to watch over her, in private as well as in public, was coming to an end at last. A visitor to the set of *Monkey Business* had been the baseball star and certified American hero, Joe

DiMaggio. If Marilyn was the dream woman of most American men, DiMaggio was the dream man. Young, handsome, charming, talented, a record-breaker with the New York Yankees but always modest and self-deprecating, Joe DiMaggio was what every red-blooded American wanted to be, and Marilyn was who they thought he deserved. She said later:

> I'd heard of Joe but didn't know much about him as I had never been interested in baseball . . . The night of our first date I was very tired but didn't like to cancel as I had promised. I kind of thought he would have slick black hair, flashy sports clothes and a New York line of patter. But he had no line at all. No jokes. He was shy and reserved, but at the same time rather warm and always friendly. I noticed that he wasn't eating the food in front of him but only staring at me. Then I noticed that I wasn't tired any more. Joe asked me to have dinner with him the next night, and the next, and the next, every night in fact until he had to leave for New York [and I never dated anyone else again].

They were not to marry until January 1954 and they were divorced on 4 October that same year, yet just as Arthur Miller was intellectually to become the keeper of Marilyn's fame, it was DiMaggio who plugged her into the heart of Middle America and who, in the long term, remained the most faithful of all her men. In many ways they were well matched, not only because they were both stars in their own right but because both had come from humble and unstable backgrounds, were largely self-educated, and were responsible for their own livelihoods. The only irony of their relationship was that their engagement lasted twice as long as their marriage.

Over the next eighteen months, while she allowed herself very slowly to be talked into a second marriage, Marilyn went on working for Fox, first in another omnibus movie, *O'Henry's Full House* (1952), in which she played a street-walker to Charles Laughton's lovable gentleman tramp, and then, reverting to high drama, *Niagara* (1953) – her eighteenth film and the first to give her top billing in a cast which also featured Joseph Cotten and Jean Peters. Not only did Marilyn sing in this picture, but she also gave a kind of serpentine performance which left the audience uncertain whether to hate her threatening sexuality or admire her survival. The *New York Times* was, however, in no doubt:

'Twentieth Century Fox have discovered the 8th and 9th wonders of the world – the grandeur of Niagara Falls and the equal grandeur of Marilyn Monroe, who may not be a perfect actress but remains the most seductive newcomer of the decade.'

In that her mother, during one of her brief periods of sanity, had been a negative cutter at RKO, Marilyn was a child of the studios. She now began to repay that debt by using a part of her weekly pay-cheque to move her mother from State institutions into the private nursing homes where she was to live long after her daughter's death, looked after by a private nurse paid for under the terms of Marilyn's will, although there is no record of loving hospital tête-à-têtes.

Years later, the novelist Norman Mailer tried to assess precisely what it was that the movie-going and fan-magazine-reading public of her time saw in Marilyn but in none of her rivals:

Marilyn always suggested that sex might be difficult and dangerous with others but would always be ice-cream with her; she looked then like a new love, ready and waiting between the sheets in the unexpected clean breath of a rare sexy morning. She was the last angel of the cinema, never made for television. She always preferred a movie theatre, with those hundreds of bodies in the dark and those wandering lights on the screen, where the luminous life of her face grew ten feet tall. . . . She knew, better than anyone, that she was the last of the myths to thrive in the long evening of the American Dream — she had been born, after all, in the year Valentino died and his footprints in the forecourt of Grauman's Chinese Theatre were the only ones that fit her feet. In the Eisenhower shank of these early 1950s, she was a cornucopia promising a future in which sex would be easy and sweet, democratic provender for everyone. Only Monroe ever suggested the purity of sexual delight. She paraded herself boldly but was never gross and her voice, carrying ripe overtones of erotic excitement, was always that of a shy young child. She was a young woman trapped in the Never-Neverland of her own curiously innocent unwariness.

She was also, of course, like another of her predecessors, Carole Lombard, that rarest of studio stars, one who could convey rampant sexiness and broad comedy at the same time. What's more, unlike Lombard, Marilyn could also sing and even dance a little. Just how well first became apparent in her next film, *Gentlemen Prefer Blondes* (1953), based on the triumphant Anita Loos Broadway musical which had made a star of the young and irrepressible Carol Channing. But for the screen it was Marilyn who played the relentlessly gold-digging Lorelei Lee and partnered Jane Russell in a Jule Styne score which included such classics as 'Diamonds are a Girl's Best Friend', 'Two Little Girls from Little Rock', and 'Bye Bye, Baby'. For the New York *Herald Tribune*, Otis Guernsey now completed his love letter to Marilyn:

> Whether singing, dancing or just staring at diamonds, this girl is irresistible and her musical is as lively as a string of firecrackers on the Fourth of July. . . . As usual, Monroe looks as though she would glow in the dark, and her version of the baby-faced blonde whose eyes only open for diamonds and close for kisses is always amusing as well as deeply alluring.

Marilyn herself was rather less romantic about her sudden arrival at superstardom. 'Well,' she said to one of her many acting coaches as they read her rave reviews, 'that's the last cock I ever have to suck.'

Some indication of how ill-prepared both she and her studio were for her triumph as Lorelei comes from a simple budgetary truth: whereas Jane Russell, as the picture's brunette, got $200,000, Marilyn got a mere $10,000. (The exact amount is not verified; others quote $150,000 and $15,000.) All that was now to change overnight. Her sense of injustice at what she saw as her undervaluation by the studio led to a long series of contract battles with Fox.

The first real dispute came when they tried to put her opposite Frank Sinatra in a remake of an old Betty Grable vehicle called *The Girl in Pink Tights*. Marilyn already had a strong sense of where she could go in pictures and the journey certainly did not involve warmed-over pieces of fluff. To put pressure on the studio bosses (and emulating Garland over at MGM) she began to appear later and later on the set, but at some cost to her own mental health. It was clear, at least to close observers, that her nerves were already somewhat frayed.

Fox did not take kindly to her refusal to make the movie, and retaliated by suspending her without pay on 4 January 1954, an echo of those not-so-distant days when they had dropped her option so unceremoniously. But by now she too knew how to play the public relations game and she played a trump card by announcing her imminent marriage to Joe DiMaggio. It was the American Dream personified. Although it has always been difficult to explain to European audiences the precise standing of DiMaggio, he was a national hero in the line that ran back to Babe Ruth and forward to the now disgraced O.J. Simpson. America's most loved sportsman was marrying Hollywood's most desired star, and the only way she could have done herself any more good would have been to marry a Kennedy or Prince Rainier of Monaco. But Marilyn was the kind of girl princes and presidents took to bed rather than to the altar, and she knew it.

They were married on 14 January 1954, in a civil ceremony at the San Francisco Justice Building: 'I wasn't even sure that I loved Joe,' she later told her faithful drama coach, Natasha Lytess, 'but I felt I ought to make everyone happy.' Immediately after the wedding, still on studio suspension, Marilyn and Joe honeymooned in Japan, where he had agreed to do a promotional tour in the baseball-mad Far East. In the middle of this working holiday, slightly bored with trailing after Joe, watching games in which she had no interest, and being ignored by a Japanese public who had no interest in her and certainly did not find her sexy or attractive, Marilyn got a summons from Bob Hope to fly to Korea to sing for American soldiers still stationed there.

For more than a week, in the low-cut, see-through dress which had made her the object of so many servicemen's dreams in *Gentlemen Prefer Blondes*, Marilyn sang to the troops, finding for the first time the joy of a live audience:

> I had never realized how famous I was until I went to Korea. That was truly the most wonderful time of my whole life. I had never seen so many men together and what's more, they were all only there to see little me on stage as I tried to sing amidst the confusion of whistles and shouts. The most wonderful thing was that wherever I looked from the stage, I could see faces smiling at me.

What day-to-day relationship with a man, even as big a star as Joe, could possibly compete with that kind of mass adoration?

On her return to Hollywood, on 24 February 1954, and a disgruntled DiMaggio, who was never really to forgive her for breaking off their honeymoon so abruptly, the marriage was already effectively over. The simple fact of being married had changed everything. It became immediately apparent that DiMaggio, from a traditional Italian American family, expected from his new bride more or less what Jim Dougherty had expected all those years before – a sexy but fundamentally homebound wife who from now on would put the spaghetti ahead of her stardom. What she had expected was that they would rise as a couple on a cloud of permanent stardom, with neither taking the upper position. What, if she thought about it at all, she expected Joe to do to remain a star after his baseball years were over, is unclear. We do know that she was shocked by his insistence on her presence by his side even when it would interfere with her shooting schedules, and the arguments that ensued were to prove the death knell of the marriage.

As if to confirm to Joe that she was never going to be happy simply as a wife, Marilyn also used these months of studio suspension to embark on a series of highly intensive acting classes with Michael Chekhov who, like Lee Strasberg in later years, was to cast himself as Svengali to her Trilby and thereby instantly set up a kind of war between himself as the representative of her career and Joe as the husband fighting to establish her private life. The tragedy of the DiMaggio marriage was its brevity. Had it survived, it is more than possible that Marilyn would also have done so. What is certain, however, is that Joe DiMaggio truly loved Marilyn and, long after her death, he arranged for red roses to be laid on her grave on every anniversary of their marriage.

Even before they were married, a photograph of Marilyn sitting up in bed, ostensibly learning her lines, appeared in the January 1953 issue of a little-known magazine called *Prevue*. What is fascinating now is to look closely at the two photographs on her bedside table. Neither is of her fiancé, Joe DiMaggio. One is of the playwright Arthur Miller, the other is of the great Italian tragedienne Eleonora Duse, already dead for fifty years. If we had been looking for pointers to Marilyn's aspirations for her future, they were there all the time.

THREE

A MILLIONAIRE

*Marilyn did not believe that diamonds were a girl's best
friend nor did she ever care how to marry a millionaire;
she was tragedy's child in that she hungered for affection
but found it only in bed — she needed security but only
found it in the arms of many different men. Marilyn was a
love addict with a craving never quite satisfied.*

Jane Ellen Wayne (John Wayne's daughter)

W hen Marilyn returned to Hollywood,
preceded by newsreel footage of her
triumphant Korean tour, it became clear that Fox
would have to bow to the public pressure of her
newfound popularity, take her off suspension, and
give her a film she really wanted to do.

Given that *Gentlemen Prefer Blondes* had already
enriched their depleted coffers by more than
$5,000,000, it was hardly surprising that the studio
should now be trying for a sequel. *How to Marry a
Millionaire* (1953), a comedy though not a musical,

was only the second film ever made in Cinema-Scope, and for this one Marilyn was given Lauren Bacall and Betty Grable as her co-stars in a shaky script by Nunnally Johnson which had all three of them seeking the moneyed men of the title. Marilyn played the near-sighted model, too vain to wear glasses while men are around, who therefore bumps into furniture and reads books upside down with a kind of limpid charm and unerring comic timing that once again proved irresistible at the box office.

Co-star Lauren Bacall kept a diary:

Betty Grable was a funny, outgoing woman, totally professional and easy. By contrast, Marilyn was frightened, insecure, trusted only her drama coach, and was always late. During our scenes she always looked at my forehead rather than my eyes. At the end of the take she'd look at her teacher standing beside the director Jean Negulesco for approval. If the headshake was no, she would insist on another take and sometimes fifteen, in all of which I had to be good as I never knew which one they would use. She was not easy, often irritating, and yet I couldn't dislike Marilyn. She had no meanness about her, no bitchery; she just concentrated on herself and the people who were there only for her. . . . She came into my dressing room one day and said where she

really wanted to be was in a San Francisco spaghetti
joint with Joe. She kept asking about my children, my
homelife with Bogie, was I happy? She seemed
wistfully envious of that aspect of my life and there
was something very sad about her wanting to reach
out, afraid to trust, always uncomfortable. She made
no effort for others and yet she was always so nice; I
think in the end she did come to trust and like me as
well as she could like anyone whose life must have
seemed to her so secure, so solved.

Although there had been no songs in *How to
Marry a Millionaire*, Marilyn was, surprisingly, to
sing no fewer than four in her next picture, her first
and only Western before *The Misfits*, on which her
career was to end only seven years later in such
despair. This first Western, *River of No Return* (1954),
was a much happier affair. Marilyn played the kind
of saloon-bar singer immortalized by Marlene
Dietrich in *Destry Rides Again* – the goodtime girl
with the wondrous voice and the golden heart
which finally teaches her both courage and nobility
in the nick of time for the fade-out in the arms of
Robert Mitchum.

The director of *River of No Return*, Otto
Preminger, recalled working with Marilyn in the

usual despairing terms that were becoming all too
familiar at this stage in her career:

> She was vulnerable and insecure, poor girl, and
> always surrounded by a little army of drama teachers
> and dressers who made enemies with all of the rest of
> us. It is maybe okay for a star to be late once or
> twice, but fifty-six times is more than the dignity of
> any director could endure. Directing Marilyn was
> like directing Lassie – you needed fourteen takes
> even to get the bloody bark right. On the other hand,
> my old Viennese aunt could always be punctual and
> learn lines – the trouble would be that nobody ever
> wanted to see her and they did queue for Marilyn.

Years later, it was to be the British playwright
Terry Johnson, in his stage fantasy *Insignificance*,
who brought together Marilyn, her husband Joe,
and the man she said she would most have wanted
to sleep with, Albert Einstein, as well as Senator Joe
McCarthy, for a play which grappled with their
iconic significance. For them all, their meaning
transcended their individual contribution to their
society, and the mention of their names still
conjures an entire world. In these middle 1950s, an
American nation still bruised by Korea, confused by

science, and bemused by McCarthyism found in Marilyn Monroe the perfect combination of knowing innocence and tough vulnerability, a confusion which went to the heart of the current mood. Not only was she entirely of her time, she had the period quality of an untouchable movie past and was on the cutting edge of the sexual revolution that was to come – before the latest incarnation of feminism, she was one of the first actresses to demand (and sulk in her tent if she did not get) control over her movies and therefore her career. It was at this time a highly unusual requirement, especially as it seemed to be coming from a dumb blonde who still appeared much less bright or calculating than she actually was. Despite her immense box-office appeal, Fox still thought of Monroe as a jumped-up tart, no better than she should be, and highly ungrateful for what she had been given.

Things were not getting any better on the domestic front either. She and Joe were now living in a rented house in Beverly Hills, still together but only just, and regularly eating out, which was, in Billy Wilder's view, much more hygienic than eating at home:

You cannot believe the state of Marilyn's house until you have seen the state of the back seat of her Cadillac. There are blouses that have been there for months, slacks, dresses, girdles, old shoes, old plane tickets, for all I know old lovers, you never saw such a filthy mess in your life and on top of it all is a whole bunch of traffic tickets. . . . Does Marilyn worry about any of this? About as much as I worry about the sun rising tomorrow.

From *River of No Return* Marilyn returned to the last of her glitzy Fox extravaganzas. *There's No Business Like Show Business* (1954) was a weary tribute to Irving Berlin which, despite an all-star cast (Ethel Merman and Donald O'Connor were billed above Marilyn with Dan Dailey, Johnny Ray and Mitzi Gaynor below her), never really lived up to the standard of its best songs. Marilyn did a very sexy version of 'Heatwave', which brought down on her unsuspecting head the wrath of Middle America – both Ed Sullivan and Hedda Hopper denounced her suggestiveness and Sullivan added: 'Monroe has now worn the welcome off this observer's mat; "Heatwave" is the most flagrant violation of good taste that this observer has ever witnessed, sickening to both me and my children.'

In private, the truth about Marilyn was that the
muddle in her house was just a symptom of the
muddle in her head. She was now on the edge of a
separation from DiMaggio, deep into psycho-
analysis, starting to drink heavily, and even debating
whether or not to run away to New York with the
new love of her life, the photographer Milton
Greene. She was still two years away from her
thirtieth birthday. The final break with Joe, whom
she always referred to as 'My Slugger', came in New
York when she was there on location for her
twenty-third film, *The Seven Year Itch* (1955). In a
famous sequence that replays on television all over
the world to this day, but never appeared in the
original cut, she stands innocently on a subway
grating while her skirt blows waist-high, displaying
the best set of legs in America and a pair (two pairs,
she insisted) of white cotton panties. The men of
New York were enchanted, Joe much less so:

> The scene was for Tom Ewell and me to come out of
> a movie house at night on Lexington Avenue; we
> stopped on a subway grating, I was wearing a sheer
> white billowy sleeveless dress which would be sent
> waist-high, revealing my legs and white panties. As
> we shot the scene a crowd gathered, among them my

Joe and his friend Walter Winchell. At first it was all innocent fun, but when Wilder kept reshooting the scene and the crowd was shouting 'Marilyn, let's see more', Joe became very upset, especially when Wilder brought the camera in close to focus on my vagina. I had put on an extra pair of panties, hoping no pubic hair would show through them but the whistles and yells of the audience became too much for Joe who shouted, 'I've had it', and stormed off into the night. For some weeks we had anyway been living in separate parts of the house in Beverly Hills and barely speaking, but after that awful night Joe just packed up and went home to San Francisco. I guess because he had long since retired from baseball he wanted me to do the same, but I still wanted a career and that was always my problem – in the end nobody ever wants to be Mr. Marilyn Monroe.

FOUR

DANCING ON THE EDGE

I shall never forget the look of death on Joe's face.

Billy Wilder

Ironically, the film which ended Marilyn's second marriage was also one of her very best. *The Seven Year Itch* (1955) was a wonderfully witty satire in the best traditions of Billy Wilder, who with this and *Some Like It Hot* (1959) was to give Marilyn the two most literate and accomplished comic scripts of her life.

So keen had Marilyn been to work with Billy Wilder that she had been willing to negotiate the deal over her previous film, *There's No Business Like Show Business* (against her instincts even accepting Donald O'Connor as a pint-sized co-star), in return for the studio promising her *The Seven Year Itch*. Of the twenty different directors she had worked for in her seven-year career, only three, John Huston, Joe

Mankiewicz and now Billy Wilder, ever really managed to penetrate her defences and overcome her neuroses sufficiently to get a really good performance out of her. She admired Huston and Mankiewicz, but Billy Wilder she genuinely trusted. In *The Seven Year Itch* she plays the television model who helps co-star Tom Ewell (repeating his original Broadway triumph as the married man whose wife is out of town for the summer, leaving him an impressionable grass widower) to realize his sexual fantasies. A fine script and a splendid performance from Ewell helped Wilder persuade Marilyn to invest the familiar dumb blonde with elements of high comedy and secret yearning, which made the film the biggest comedy hit of its year.

'I shall never forget', said Wilder, thinking back to the fatal night of the subway-grating incident, 'the look of death on Joe's face.' And sure enough, on 5 October 1954, while they were still shooting *The Seven Year Itch*, the divorce lawyer Jerry Geisler announced that, after nine months, the American Dream Couple were single again. The official reason on the divorce decree was given as 'incompatibility', and Marilyn added, by way of explanation:

He didn't talk to me. He was cold. He was indifferent to me as a human being and as an artist. He didn't want me to have friends of my own. He didn't want me to do my work. He watched television instead of talking to me. Joe distrusts everybody in Hollywood except Frank Sinatra; we just lived in two quite different worlds. He went for days without even speaking to me. He's the moodiest man I have ever met.

A month later, with *The Seven Year Itch* safely in the can, Marilyn made the first of what would be her increasingly frequent visits to the Cedars of Lebanon Hospital for what was described as 'minor internal surgery'. Over the next few years, the number of press photographs of Marilyn either going into or coming out of some kind of clinic would be exceeded only by those of Elizabeth Taylor on her almost weekly hospital circuit.

On New Year's Day 1955, with an impressively theatrical sense of timing, Marilyn called a press conference to announce the birth of the New Monroe. Conveniently overlooking the fact that she still owed Fox several pictures under an existing contract, she announced that henceforth she would only be working for herself as Marilyn Monroe

Productions, a new company of which the other directors were to be her lover, Milton Greene, and Paula and Lee Strasberg, husband and wife directors of the Actors' Studio, the centre of the Stanislavsky-based 'Method' school of acting in New York, one which had already attracted the young Marlon Brando and Eli Wallach, among many others, including her old friend Shelley Winters. The reason for this, Marilyn told the press, was:

> So I can play the better kind of roles I now want. I don't like a lot of my previous pictures, I'm tired of sex roles and I want to broaden my scope by doing real dramatic parts. There's no point in doing the same thing over and over again. I want to keep growing as a person and an actress but in Hollywood they never ask my opinion, they just tell me what time to come to work tomorrow.

True, the newly serious Marilyn did not get her rebirth off to the most plausible start by appearing for a benefit a few weeks later in an if-you've-got-it-flaunt-it costume on a bejewelled elephant at Madison Square. 'I don't want to be a freak,' she then said, carefully distancing herself from the rest of that particular circus.

Staying now in New York, she began at last to mix with the kind of Manhattan intellectuals whose company she craved as an alternative to the dimwits of Hollywood. At the nightclub El Morocco she danced with Truman Capote, who would write of her:

> Marilyn is not in any traditional sense an actress at all. What she has, a presence, a luminosity, a flickering intelligence, is so fragile and subtle that it could never surface on stage. It can only be caught by the camera, but anyone who thinks that she is nothing more than another Harlow or harlot is totally mad.

Although she showed no desire to return to Hollywood, and although their divorce was now legally complete, Joe suddenly turned up at the June premiere of *The Seven Year Itch*, which coincided with Marilyn's twenty-ninth birthday. Could this, they were asked by the press, mean a reconciliation? 'Well, honey, what do you think?' asked Joe, only to have his ex-wife humiliatingly reply in public, 'No, honey, just call it a visit'. A few days later, still in the throes of her love affair with Manhattan and the Actors' Studio, Marilyn met at a party there the man whose photograph had been on her bedside table for the last five years – playwright Arthur Miller, who was to become her third and last husband.

Miller was, even then, one of the most successful of all American playwrights but, despite tremendous critical triumphs with plays such as *All My Sons* and *Death of a Salesman*, he did not become an icon until he defied the modern witchhunts of the McCarthy anti-Communist tribunal in 1953 by writing *The Crucible*. When he met Marilyn in 1955, it was against this background of intellectual respect, almost adoration, among an entire group of writers and artists who had been or were afraid of being persecuted by the House Un-American Activities Committee but had lacked his courage to fight back. He was also many years into a rather dull marriage which was all but over.

It is hardly surprising that Marilyn would be attracted to a man whose preoccupation in his plays is always centrally about characters coming face to face with themselves. We know that the lonely young movie star read voraciously while waiting for her 'takes' (although, as Miller was later to notice, she never actually finished a book – 'She somehow always just got the idea of it and that for her was enough') and we have already noted her passion for self-improvement and the need for an education her peripatetic childhood had not provided. Who better to arrive in her life than the strong man of the American theatre?

Miller describes in his memoirs his first impressions.

> She always seemed more like a prop than an actress . . . the quintessential dumb blonde on the arm of worldly and corrupt representatives of Hollywood society.
>
> In a roomful of actresses and the wives of substantial men, all striving to dress and behave with emphatically ladylike reserve, Marilyn Monroe seemed almost ludicrously provocative, a strange bird in the aviary if only because her dress was so blatantly tight, declaring rather than insinuating that she had brought her body along and that it was the best in the room. . . . It was a perfection that aroused the wish to defend it, though I suspected even at the time how tough she must be to have survived Hollywood for so long and with such relative success; but apparently she was now alone in the world.

She was also devastated by the death of her mentor Johnny Hyde, and the fact that his family would not even allow her into his hospital room. Starting her new life in New York, with Milton Greene now taking Hyde's place as her surrogate father, Marilyn unwisely announced to a cynical press her desire to play Grushenka in the film of Dostoevsky's *The Brothers Karamazov*, at a time when most observers thought quite wrongly that she couldn't even spell, let alone play, so intellectually demanding a character. By now she was taking almost daily lessons at the Actors' Studio and quarrelling again with Fox, who soon suspended her for turning down yet another mindless sex comedy, this one entitled *How to Be Very Popular*. The role went to Betty Grable and effectively finished her career.

For Marilyn, the truth was that in New York, with her acting classes, her budding friendship with Miller which turned rapidly into an affair, and her discovery of the theatre and a whole generation of stage actors, her life had taken a sharp turn away from the old Hollywood routines. But California was not to forgive such apparent treachery. First, fan magazines tried to nail her on the grounds that she was now befriending many undesirable East Coast intellectuals and closet Communists, and then the scandal rag *Confidential* got hold of something

Marilyn Monroe dancing with Dan Dailey in the unsuccessful 1950 musical western *A Ticket to Tomahawk*. (20th Century Fox: courtesy Kobal)

In 1950 Marilyn played in a night-club scene with Dick Powell in the film *Right Cross*. (MGM: courtesy Kobal)

A poster for the film *As Young as You Feel*, in which Marilyn played a glamorous secretary. (20th Century Fox: courtesy Kobal)

MacDonald Carey, Marilyn, Zachary Scott and Claudette Colbert in a scene from the 1951 film *Let's Make It Legal*. Once again, Marilyn played a gold-digging blonde. (20th Century Fox: courtesy Kobal)

Marilyn posing for the camera during the filming of the 1953 film *Niagara*. This was her eighteenth film, and the first in which she received top billing. (20th Century Fox: courtesy Kobal)

Jane Russell and Marilyn Monroe in the 1953 film *Gentlemen Prefer Blondes*, also starring Elliott Reed and Tommy Noonan. This film demonstrated her talents as a singer and dancer in the part of Lorelei Lee, the 'relentless gold digger' and brought her to superstardom. (20th Century Fox: courtesy Kobal)

Marilyn on the set of the comedy *How to Marry a Millionaire*, in which she starred with Betty Grable and Lauren Bacall. In her diary, Lauren Bacall described Marilyn as 'frightened, insecure . . . and always late. . . . there was something very sad about her wanting to reach out, afraid to trust, always uncomfortable'. (20th Century Fox: courtesy Kobal)

Marilyn with Joe DiMaggio, her second husband, whom she married on 14 January 1954.
(*Illustrated London News*)

Marilyn starred with Robert Mitchum in the western *River of No Return*, in 1954.
(20th Century Fox: courtesy Kobal)

Later in 1954 Marilyn starred in the musical *There's No Business Like Show Business*, but was attacked for her sexy rendition of 'Heatwave': Ed Sullivan described it as 'the most flagrant violation of good taste'. (20th Century Fox: courtesy Kobal)

Marilyn with her third husband, the playwright Arthur Miller, pictured here in 1959 when she was in London to film *The Prince and the Showgirl* with Laurence Olivier. (Photo: Jack Cardiff/ Camera Press, London)

Marilyn Monroe pictured outside her home in Englefield Green in July 1956, shortly after her marriage to Arthur Miller. (Hulton Getty Picture Collection Limited)

One of Marilyn's best known and most successful films was the 1959 comedy *Some Like It Hot*, in which she starred with Tony Curtis and Jack Lemmon. Tony Curtis famously remarked that kissing Marilyn was like kissing Hitler. (United Artists: Ronald Grant Archive)

A scene from *Some Like It Hot*, with Jack Lemmon and Tony Curtis in drag hiding in an all-girl orchestra to escape the Mob. (United Artists: courtesy Kobal)

very much worse. 'Marilyn is Blonde Who Traded Pills with Director Nicholas Ray' was the first public reference to her drug problem, and the more Marilyn tried to distance herself from the studios the more they seemed determined to destroy what they had so carefully created. In fact, despite her enormous box-office appeal, Marilyn had never been a studio favourite. Nobody much wanted to do her any favours, and Fox raised not a single finger to quash the damage being done by a baying fan press. She was unprotected even by those for whom she had made so much money.

For Marilyn, as for Miller, there was now a strong sense of exile, and early in 1956 they called a press conference to announce that, as soon as possible, they would be leaving for Europe to work with Sir Laurence Olivier on a prestigious Terence Rattigan screen adaptation of his play *The Sleeping Prince*. Olivier had already played this on stage, in the death throes of his marriage to Vivien Leigh, whom he was now replacing, on screen at any rate, with Marilyn. Before that could happen, her Marilyn Monroe Productions reached an uneasy kind of truce with Fox, whereby she agreed to give them one more film on their own territory.

For Marilyn this was a great break. The picture she was offered was to be a screen adaptation of William Inge's long-running Broadway hit *Bus Stop* (1956), in which a group of unrelated travellers, trapped in a tawdry truck stop during a snowstorm, play out a human comedy of heartbreaking reality. Each stranded passenger has a tragic or funny reason for wanting to get back on the bus, and Marilyn was to play the role (created on stage by Kim Stanley) of a hopeful but untalented singer trying for the big-time in the big city if only she could get there.

She set off for Hollywood reluctantly because this meant that she would now be separated from Miller, whose work kept him in the East, but they remained in nightly telephone touch and Arthur was later to write of her feelings of inadequacy working with Joshua Logan, the film's director:

I was now hearing from her a new terror, an abandoned voice crying out to a deaf sky, and the dead miles between us choked me with frustration . . . she was dancing on the edge and the drop down was forever. . . . 'Oh Papa,' she would say, 'I can't make it, I can't make it' and suddenly suicide leapt up before me, an act I had never connected with her until then. . . . Once this picture was done we would marry and start a new and real life. 'I don't want this any more, Papa, I can't fight them alone, I want to live with you in the country and be a good wife, and if somebody wants me for a wonderful picture . . .'

In spite of her doubts about Logan, her ability to carry an important film, the conflict between her desire to run away to the country and her need to prove her intellectual and artistic equality, and the ever more frequent panic attacks which sent her back to the pillbox and the bottle, *Bus Stop* was what persuaded Fox to sign her to a new four-picture contract, in collaboration with her own new company and worth an unprecedented $8,000,000. Moreover, Logan had nothing but admiration for her:

> She was a combination of Chaplin and Garbo – always the most beautiful person in the room, and certainly the most fun – warm, witty and with the enthusiasm of a child. Innocent, yes, but never ignorant, stupid or gross. She was never able to feel the respect she most longed for but at this time she had reached the peak of her emotional and intellectual life.

And although the Academy of Motion Picture Arts

and Sciences refused her even an Oscar nomination, there was no doubt among the critics that she had finally proved herself a great actress. The *Saturday Review* wrote:

> What she does here is unquestionably the most difficult feat for any film personality. She submerges herself so completely in the role of Inge's Hollywood hopeful 'chantootsie' from the Ozarks that one searches in vain for glimpses of the former calendar pin-up. . . . There is pathos, humour and a desperate pride about this girl and Monroe brings her completely to life.

As soon as shooting was complete and Arthur had collected his divorce from Reno on 11 June 1956, he and Marilyn were married on 1 July 1956 at Roxbury, Connecticut, the home of Arthur's parents and where he still lives. This was, said the press, the wedding of 'The Egghead and The Hourglass', and Marilyn, ever eager to throw herself into every new role, private or public, duly converted to the Jewish faith. Even before they were married, Miller was already wondering what he was getting himself into, and was concerned that he would not be able to hold all the pieces of the ever more fragile and desperately damaged Marilyn together. Fearful that a refusal to go through with the marriage would destroy her utterly, he did turn up for the ceremony but without great confidence in the longevity of the match.

FIVE

'NOBODY'S PERFECT'

Come on, Darling, be sexy.

Laurence Olivier

On 13 July 1956 Marilyn and Arthur were on the plane to London to meet up with the Oliviers and start pre-production on what was now to be called *The Prince and the Showgirl*. For once, the timing was totally right; Miller had the first London production of his *A View from the Bridge* to oversee, and was as eager to distance himself from the McCarthyite politics of Washington as was Marilyn to get away from the inane publicity of Hollywood. Back with Miller, Marilyn was much more secure and the demons had temporarily fled in the euphoria of having married the man she thought would keep them away forever.

Entire books (not least the wondrously revealing

diaries of Alan Clark's brother Colin who was a runner on the set) have been written about the making of *The Prince and the Showgirl*, one of those films that turned out to be vastly more interesting behind the cameras than it ever was on the screen. The newly-wed happiness of the Millers contrasted sharply with the crumbling marriage of the Oliviers, especially as Vivien Leigh was understandably resentful at having been displaced from the role she had created and for which she had been rather more plausibly cast, by the younger blonde with her stronger box-office appeal and her adoring husband.

Rattigan's always flimsy plot, originally written three years earlier as a coronation vehicle for the Oliviers, was set in London at the time of an earlier coronation, that of King George V in 1912. The prince of the title was a lovelorn Ruritanian monarch who falls hopelessly in love with a (now American) showgirl in a plot that might have been helped by an Ivor Novello score.

In a curious way, although the film itself did nobody much good, it led indirectly to the whole of Laurence Olivier's late-life career. During the shooting it was Arthur Miller who persuaded Olivier to go back to the Royal Court and take a second look at *Look Back in Anger*, a play the actor-knight had originally hated. Shown by Miller the strength of this new way of looking at theatre writing, Olivier asked John Osborne, the play's author, to write a script for him. The result was the ground-breaking *The Entertainer*, and an entirely different Olivier, one more connected to the fabric of the contemporary theatre, was born.

But back on the set, things rapidly went from bad to worse. Olivier, much to Marilyn's uneasiness, was also directing the film and although Josh Logan had hailed this new star partnership as 'the most exciting combination since black and white', it proved to be nothing of the kind. Marilyn, surrounded as usual by her army of supporters and hangers-on, led by Paula Strasberg and Milton Greene, would only ever accept Olivier's direction if they endorsed it.

She took, as always, to arriving on the set later and later, and morale on the studio floor was so low that several of the actors actually held a protest meeting to state their unhappiness with what they saw as Marilyn's persistent unprofessionalism. They even suggested that she be replaced with Vivien until the voice of sanity was heard from the oldest trouper in the film, Dame Sybil Thorndike, playing the Queen Mother. 'Just one little problem if you sack darling Marilyn,' she said. 'Of all of us on this film she is the only one with the faintest idea how to act in front of a camera.'

Olivier, now desperately unhappy with Marilyn on the set and Vivien at home, still had no real idea of what Marilyn could offer an audience; 'Come on, Darling, be sexy' was not much help by way of advice, and in retaliation Marilyn now took to calling him 'Mister Sir'. Once again it was Dame Sybil who instinctively understood everything that Marilyn was about. 'Don't look at her on the set,' she advised Olivier, 'look at her in the rushes – that's where she comes to life. She has an innocence which is quite extraordinary – even when playing a brazen hussy it always comes out an innocent young girl.'

But he couldn't take this excellent advice, either as director or as co-star. He didn't even try to understand Marilyn's dependence on her entourage and his deep distrust of the Method did not endear him to anyone in the Marilyn camp. Their relationship deteriorated to the point where they were only speaking through intermediaries. His position was later summarized by an observer on the set:

> Marilyn has an absolutely unconscious but basic resistance to acting. She loves to show herself, loves to be a star, loves all the success side of it. But to be an actress is something she does not really want at all, and they were wrong to try and make one of her. Her wit, her adorable charm, her sex appeal and her bewitching personality are all part of her, but they are not to be associated with any art or talent.

This was only partially true at best, but it does seem to encapsulate the feelings of the British cast and crew about Marilyn, who was cordially disliked on the film, a dislike which communicated itself to the public.

Press reaction to *The Prince and the Showgirl* was little short of catastrophic on both sides of the Atlantic. What had been originally cooked as a soufflé finished up as suet pudding, with Olivier looking pained and embarrassed while Marilyn's usual showgirl with the heart of pure tinsel was also getting a little tarnished around the edges. For British audiences, the only headline-worthy or dramatic thing about *The Prince and the Showgirl* had

been Marilyn's broken shoulder strap at one of the
early press conferences.

While they were living in England, in that
summer of 1956, Miller was served with a
subpoena demanding that he present himself in
Washington DC to answer Contempt of Congress
charges for having refused to name names of other
left-wing artists and writers with whom he had
attended a Communist Party meeting in 1947.
Although he had signed an anti-Communist oath in
order to get a passport to travel to England, the
committee routed by his previous testimony was
still out to get him. Two months after their return
to New York at the end of 1956, he was convicted
on two counts of contempt, each carrying a
maximum sentence of $1,000 and one year in jail.
After several more months of negotiation, Miller
finally received a thirty-day suspended sentence and
a $500 fine, though two years later, by which time
the McCarthyite feeding frenzy had ended, even this
reduced penalty was reversed on appeal.

Determined now to be the wife and mother she
had always promised herself and three husbands that
she would be, most of the next eighteen months of
Marilyn's life were taken up with a succession of

three ectopic pregnancies; their effect on her always fragile mental health was severe. Her tragic inability to have children would haunt and further damage her for the last five years of her life.

Marilyn was now, for the first time, rather at a loose end. Without the possibility of children to occupy her, and with Arthur hard at work on what would become an original screenplay for her, she drifted about New York and Connecticut without any clear plan. She turned down both *Can-Can* and *Some Came Running*, both of which went instead to Shirley MacLaine. Her coveted role of Grushenka in *The Brothers Karamazov* went to Maria Schell, and Marilyn spent those months reading, and making the occasional radio or television appearance. It was time to go back to work.

The script which did finally tempt her back to Hollywood came inevitably from her favourite director, Billy Wilder, in July 1958. *Some Like It Hot* was a madcap comedy about two petty crooks hiding from the Mob in an all-girl orchestra after they have unwittingly witnessed the St Valentine's Day Massacre. The crooks were Tony Curtis and Jack Lemmon, while Marilyn's character was the innocent girl singer who goes through most of the film believing that her two best friends are, in fact, women. The entire joke rests on Marilyn's ability to convince the audience that she can exchange 'girly' secrets with two bruisers and still not know the truth. All those dumb blonde roles pay off for Marilyn in *Some Like It Hot*. Who else could act such a role well enough to turn an entire genre on its head? The *double entendres*, the fluffy non sequiturs, the wide-eyed innocence is all heartland Marilyn, but here she had the chance to demonstrate that she knew exactly what she was doing.

The rest of the cast featured such long-forgotten stars as George Raft, Pat O'Brien and Joe E. Brown, and part of Wilder's brilliance in the film is to satirise precisely the kind of films for which these actors were most familiar. Only Marilyn could have taken those elements and been miserable enough with the process to make a hell of her own life and that of everyone else on the picture.

Marilyn's real unhappiness about her role as Sugar Kane arose when she realized that hers was by no means the best part in the picture, and she never forgave Jack Lemmon for replacing Frank Sinatra, the actor she had originally wanted in the role. 'You have to be orderly', explained Wilder, 'in order to shoot disorder and this was the best disorder I ever had.' Nevertheless, filming was a nightmare for all concerned. First of all, in a complex tax manoeuvre, there were to be about five producers, including Monroe herself who deeply disapproved of the others' decision to make the film in black and white. Marilyn knew that she always looked better in colour, but Wilder's problem was that Lemmon and Curtis would only be believable in full drag if the whole picture was shot in monochrome.

When the filming started, she retaliated in her usual way, arriving later and later on the set until she would solemnly appear in full costume at 6 pm, just after Wilder had dismissed the crew. He said:

The real question is whether Marilyn is a person at all – she has breasts like granite, she defies gravity, and her brain, like Swiss cheese, is full of holes. She hasn't the vaguest concept of time or day; she will arrive late and tell you she couldn't find the studio, despite the fact that she had been working there for fifteen years. She is one of the wonderful rascals of this world and I only hope she never gets straightened out by all those analysts of hers – if she does she will be a clenched and dreary thing. As for me, both my doctor and my psychiatrist tell me I am too old and too rich

ever to go through this kind of thing again – it took
me weeks after the shooting for me not to want,
every day, to beat up my own wife, so strongly had
Marilyn made me hate her sex.

Others involved were no more complimentary.
Tony Curtis said that kissing Marilyn was just like
kissing Hitler, an opinion which was certainly
coloured by how much trouble she was now having
in getting out of bed in the morning. It once took
her forty takes to deliver the single line, 'Where's
the bourbon?', even though Wilder had pasted the
words on to the drinks cupboard for her; another
single line of her dialogue, 'It's me, Sugar', took her
a record sixty-one takes. Not surprisingly, *Some Like
It Hot* went nearly a million dollars over budget and
several weeks over its shooting schedule. Ironically,
after her death three years later, this was the only
one of her pictures which managed posthumously to
pay off all her debts. Her net profit reached more
than $3,000,000.

And the following March (1959), by one of those
unlikely miracles which fill the annals of Hollywood
history, the picture opened to rave reviews, five
Oscar nominations and a profit of some $5,000,000.

It was, noted Wilder, quite simply the biggest hit that any of them had ever known.

As for Marilyn's behaviour on-set, as Joe E. Brown says, in the classic fade-out of the picture, 'Well, nobody's perfect'.

SIX

SELF-DESTRUCTION

*It was as though the tide had turned in her life and was
already beginning to run out.*

John Huston

For Arthur Miller, Marilyn was now not just a
wife but a full-time occupation. Increasingly
aware that, if there was a key to her despair, he did
not possess it, he devoted himself to giving her the
kind of emotional support that she had never known
before, and even to work as a kind of script doctor,
on whatever lines she was trying to learn at the
time.

> This was a bad miscalculation, bringing us no closer
> to each other. She seemed to take for granted my
> sacrifice of great blocks of my time, and if it was
> plain that her inner desperation was never going to
> let up, it was equally clear that literally nothing I
> knew how to do could slow its destructive progress.

In the last three years of her life, Marilyn seemed hell-bent on self-destruction despite having finally found a distinguished writer to love and marry her and movies which at last did not seem to be a waste of her remarkable talents. During the shooting of *Some Like It Hot* she had lost yet another baby, and her miscarriage caused a full-scale telegram battle between Wilder and Miller, after the director had made public his contempt for Marilyn's apparently lackadaisical working habits:

> Now [wired Miller to Wilder] that the hit for which she is so largely responsible is in your hands and its income to you assured, your attack upon my wife is contemptible, unjust and cruel. My only solace is that, despite you, her beauty and her humanity shine through as they always have.

Wilder immediately cabled in reply:

> Of course I am deeply sorry that Marilyn lost her baby. But I must reject your implication that overwork or inconsiderate treatment by me or anyone else on the set was in any way responsible. The fact is that the studio pampered her, coddled her, and acceded to all of her whims. The only one to show any lack of consideration was Marilyn herself in

Self-destruction

her treatment of her co-stars and co-workers. Right from the first day, before there was any hint of her pregnancy, her chronic tardiness and unpreparedness cost us 18 shooting days, hundreds of thousands of dollars and countless heartaches.

Somewhere inside his head Miller knew the wily old director was right. But he had devoted himself to 'fixing' Marilyn, so her continued failure became his, and he was still not ready to admit that he was not and could never be the answer to her problems; and nor, for that matter, could he admit that her depression could not be lifted by work either, because seldom in the whole history of Hollywood can a film made with such rancour have turned out to be such a worldwide smash-hit. *Variety* loved everything about it:

Some Like It Hot, directed in masterly style by Billy Wider, is probably the funniest picture of recent memory. It's a whacky, clever, farcical comedy that starts off like a firecracker and keeps on throwing off lively sparks till the very end. . . . To coin a phrase, Marilyn has never looked better. Her performance as 'Sugar' has a deliciously naive quality. She's a comedienne with that combination of sex appeal and timing that just can't be beat.

And Archer Winston in the *New York Post* spoke for critics from Teheran to Timbuctoo: 'To get down to cases, Marilyn does herself proud, giving a performance of such intrinsic quality that you begin to believe she's only being herself and it is herself who fits into that distant period and this picture so well.'

Some Like It Hot was a triumph for cast, crew, company and studio. But despite the critical euphoria and unanimous agreement that Marilyn had given the performance of her career, as both dumb blonde and talented comedienne, her masters at Fox were unable to come up with a follow-up script she might be willing to take on. Even with one of the world's greatest playwrights as her in-house script doctor, she rejected all the ideas lobbed over her transom by the studio who had put up with her tantrums, tardiness and terrorizing for the past ten years.

She turned down *The Sound and the Fury* but, surprisingly, did agree at the beginning of 1959 to play yet another showgirl, Amanda Dell, in a disastrously underwritten musical satire called *Let's Make Love*. In view of the enormous abuse she was by then wreaking on her body from pill bottles and vodka bottles, it is astonishing that her stock in trade, the most beautiful and voluptuous figure in the history of the cinema, was still as perfectly formed as ever. You can't play a showgirl with bulges and Marilyn didn't have any. The ravages of her self-destruction were apparent only in the very occasional glimpses of her haunted eyes and lank hair as she entered or left yet another clinic.

Meanwhile her own especial currency, though still miraculously intact, was being rapidly devalued. Studio moguls bored with the constant off-screen dramas and alarums, which were a normal part of working with Marilyn, began casting around for an easier option. They had already come up with such Marilyn clones as Jayne Mansfield, Sherree North and Mamie van Doren, while even Britain's own sweater-girl, Diana Dors, was briefly considered as a substitute Marilyn, so desperate was Fox to escape from under what had clearly become a no-win situation all round.

Marilyn returned to New York and the Actors' Studio, determined to maintain her distance and thereby raise her stock to its accustomed stratosphere. In her more lucid moments she had no doubt that she could see off the competition and demonstrate that there was only one Marilyn Monroe.

But her marriage to Arthur Miller was beginning to crumble. Despite everything he had done to try to help her, even putting his own writing into abeyance to provide the support she soaked up like some exotic sponge, emerging every time still needier and more desperate, Marilyn was sinking further and further into her own fears, staring daily into an abyss from which no amount of love, compassion, psychiatry or reassurance could remove her. She and Arthur no longer had the give and take of a marriage of adults; their relationship was now reduced to the exclusive giving of one and the neurotic taking of the other, until neither could remember the equality of the different star-qualities which had brought them together.

Let's Make Love should have been a much better movie than it turned out to be. It had a wonderful cast and in George Cukor an experienced director who was famous for retrieving the careers of troubled female stars, from Katharine Hepburn to Joan Crawford. In addition to co-stars Tony Randall and Yves Montand, Marilyn had a supporting cast that included Wilfrid Hyde White and Frankie

Vaughan (in his only Hollywood picture) and three guest-star cameos played by Gene Kelly, Bing Crosby and Milton Berle as the experts hired by Montand to teach him to dance, sing and clown in order to win the heart of Marilyn. Playing Clement, a billionaire desperate to break into show business and thereby get closer to Marilyn's Amanda, Yves Montand was an inspired choice but very far from the first: the original idea for the casting was to have a Gregory Peck, Rock Hudson, James Stewart, Gary Cooper figure, so wooden that his inability to perform would be all the more hilarious. When, however, and in retrospect wisely, all these stars turned it down, Cukor ended up with Yves Montand, a French song and dance man as well as a great actor who had nearly as much trouble making himself look clumsy and incompetent as he did with the language, this being his first non-French film. And that was just the beginning of the troubles with Yves.

It was his wife, Simone Signoret, whose English was nearly perfect, who read the script and encouraged her husband to go for Hollywood stardom. Ironically, what was to become a heavily publicized affair between Marilyn and her leading man nearly destroyed the Montands' marriage and did in fact finally finish off the ailing Monroe/Miller union. Arthur Miller had known both Montand and Signoret for many years, since they had both starred in the original French stage and screen versions of *The Crucible* (as *Les Sorcières de Salem*). But his memoirs make no reference to Marilyn's last major show business affair.

At first, the Millers and the Montands were an inseparable quartet around town. As left-wing intellectuals in a still fervently right-wing city, they clearly had more than *The Crucible* in common already, and theirs still was the company Marilyn most cherished after the inanities of the Hollywood gossip which was all around her. But the production was slowed down by an actors' strike, during which Simone had to leave for a film commitment in Europe and Arthur was due in New York for discussions about a new play. Left to each other in a town neither liked, and ensconced in adjacent bungalows at the Beverly Hills Hotel with little to do but wait for the strike to end, the inevitable happened between Marilyn and Yves.

In the end, it was Signoret who summarized this disastrous Montand/Miller liaison with elegance and grace:

The American press desperately wanted the four of us (Marilyn, Montand, Miller and myself) to play parts we had never learned in a play that we never even read. In truth, there was nothing resembling the blonde heartbreaker or the moody dark Frenchmen or the bookworm or the admirable wife standing on her dignity which were the labels they pasted on us afterwards. And it's a pity too that Arthur Miller, of whom I was once very fond, chose to write *After the Fall* about Marilyn after her death.

If the Millers and the Montands were at this time bound together by anything, it was their general unpopularity in Middle America. Montand, like Miller, had been in trouble with the State Department for his supposed Communism and Marilyn, as if hell-bent on yet another kind of self-destruction, now gave an interview to a Hollywood gossip columnist in which she announced of her fellow stars: 'Rock Hudson is too effeminate, he sits around sewing lace curtains; Gregory Peck is just too tall and Tony Perkins is a sadistic boy who likes terrifying old ladies.' She added, for good measure, that she would have been a far better choice for *Cleopatra* than Elizabeth Taylor, and that Judy Garland was altogether too neurotic for her own good. To say all this about five of the most bankable of all Hollywood stars was one quote too far for the majority of the movie-going public. For the already semi-detached Marilyn to complain about a fellow actor's neurosis was seen as the folly that it clearly was.

As for Yves Montand, although accused by many of simply trying to boost his Hollywood career with Marilyn, there was no doubt that, like everyone who ever got close to her, he too soon wished to become her guardian angel. Several years after her death he wrote:

In Marilyn there was without doubt a constant and obsessive awareness of her own limitations, the conviction that she was never to become the great actress she so longed to be. But she had an immense character, and an extremely strong nature, even though in life as on the screen, she had that 'little girl voice'. The fascination she exercised and her seductive power were present almost without her knowing it, whether she used them or not. She had no need to check the seam of her stockings to give a man ideas; whether she talked about the rain or the fine weather or the studio cafeteria menu she had the same power. She had a kind of innocence and the less she tried, the more attractive she was. Marilyn was a being apart, in the sense that it was her own inner light that drove her into the spotlight. If I believed in God, I would say that God alone could generate such a light – a light beyond the control of those in whom it burns. Marilyn suffered at not being recognized as a real actress, but she was not really an actress at all; she existed somewhere far beyond mere enactment.

This was the first time that Montand had cheated on Signoret, and as soon as *Let's Make Love* wrapped, he returned to a forgiving wife. Like most of Marilyn's relationships this one ended leaving her worse off than her partner. While the Montands went through a sticky patch, the Millers were rent asunder permanently. It must have seemed to Marilyn that she destroyed every important relationship in her life and that the men who on the one hand could not keep their hands off her, on the other found her altogether too much trouble, and they all, sooner rather than later, headed for the hills.

SEVEN

THE MISFITS

The Misfits *is an attempt at the ultimate motion picture.*

Frank Taylor (Producer)

By June 1960 Marilyn was, yet again, on her own, her already meagre emotional resources stretched thinner than ever. Distraught and distressed, she now faced a new problem. Although her marriage to Miller was effectively over, the two of them were still locked together by one screenplay. Throughout their partnership, Miller had planned one great gift to his wife, an original script written expressly for her which would at last make real the dream she had always most cherished – that of being taken seriously as a major dramatic film star.

The script he had been working on for her over these last two years was, with a terrible irony, to be called *The Misfits*. It would tell the story of a young divorcee meeting up with an old cowboy and a worn-out rodeo rider for a last round-up of some horses doomed to slaughter. What Miller saw in this was a lament for the end of the old West. *The Misfits* of the title were both the horses and their would-be rescuers and a long, complex narrative was shot through with a sense of loneliness and despair which came from somewhere deep in Miller's increasing certainty that everything he valued was now at an end. This tremendous sense of bleak finality was heightened by the casting of Clark Gable, only months before his death, as the old cowboy, and the already drugged and doomed Montgomery Clift as the worn-out rodeo rider. The director was their old friend John Huston, who had worked with Marilyn ten years earlier on her first dramatic screen appearance in *The Asphalt Jungle*.

Now, as they came together for the shoot, Huston realized that something had gone very wrong with her:

> She seemed already to be caught in a fast downward spiral. This was already the beginning of her end and it came all too quickly. She took so many sleeping pills at night that she needed stimulants to wake her up in the morning and this ravaged the girl. She broke down and I had to send her to a hospital for a week in which we interrupted the shooting.

The Misfits was, like the later *Heaven's Gate*, one of those pictures on which most of the drama happened behind the cameras, and although Marilyn had some charming and tender moments with Gable, another of the father figures she had always sought, there was no salvation ahead. In the relentless heat of the Nevada desert in the July of 1960 Marilyn, her marriage, Gable, Clift and the film itself all began to fall apart more or less in unison.

In its time, *The Misfits* was the most expensive black-and-white movie ever made and even by the usual Huston standards of really tough locations (*The African Queen*, *The Night of the Iguana*, *The Red Badge of Courage*) this one was the worst, and the survivors, of which there were few, deserved medals for gallantry.

At times, Monroe and Clift were taking so many drugs that they were incapable of working for days at a time; Gable was in agony with a bad back and worried about the pregnancy of his young wife, who tragically was to give birth to their son only after his death. He died a week after the film was completed, and for years afterwards it was accused of causing his death. The general air of gloom on the picture and the sense that it was spinning inexorably out of control affected everybody. Marilyn, especially, was non-functional for nearly the entire shooting schedule.

Miller, meanwhile, a lugubrious presence on the set where Marilyn's ever-present band of Strasberg cronies would shout abuse at him, was equally unhappy until mid-way through the shooting, when a young photographer came to take some stills and brought with her the serenity, common sense and light-heartedness for which Inge Morath is still famous. It must have been a welcome breath of fresh air entering a foetid atmosphere, and she was able to lighten the mood at least during her brief stay in Nevada. She and Arthur did not get together for several years after *The Misfits* but, once they did, they remained together permanently. Miller and Monroe were married for barely four years but his union with Inge Morath has lasted for more than thirty, during which she has become one of the world's greatest portrait photographers and he has continued to write plays which will surely contribute to the future definition of this century's theatre.

Marilyn was now under a greater strain than even she had ever known before, but, as always, the story depends on the storyteller. Miller's tale could be summarized as that of a loyal, hard-working intellectual who, out of his passionate love for Marilyn, had given her some of the best years of his working life and received little in return beyond hysteria and infidelity. Marilyn's supporters would suggest a rather different story, that she had raised him for the first time to her level of fame, that she had stood by him and indeed paid his legal costs through some very difficult political times, and that the House Un-American Activities Committee had decided not to pursue him on the grounds that the publicity he received as her husband made him too hot to handle.

Their very different needs – his for peace, hers for stimulation – were exacerbated by her mental health problems and his contempt for the triviality of her preoccupations. At one time they loved each other very much, but it is possible that they never liked one another at all. What is sure is that, following the initial intense attraction of opposites when each believed that the other was the answer to their every dream, a fantasy which lasted a relatively short time, they had a terrible marriage in which, whoever was at fault on any particular day, the individual needs of each exaggerated the differences between them.

Shooting on *The Misfits* wrapped on 5 November 1960, with Gable and Marilyn driving away through the desert as he says, 'Just head for that big star'. A day later, Gable had the massive heart attack which was to kill him the following week, and already the national press, alerted by several location crises, were eagerly reporting that the film would turn out to be a total disaster. In retrospect, however, it is nothing of the kind. *The Misfits* is a haunting lament not only for the values of the old West but also for the kind of superstar performances from Monroe, Gable and Clift which were all too soon to disappear with them, leaving Hollywood a smaller and still sadder place.

But Marilyn now had to get on with her own life. Her frequent visits to clinics, which had once been for her regular miscarriages, were now invariably occasioned by drug overdoses and a series of low-key suicide attempts from which at this time no one doubted she expected to be rescued. Her terror of aging, her fear of going as crazy as her mother, and her feeling of total failure at being unable to carry a pregnancy through to term were all now subsumed by a new and potentially very dangerous affair.

On 20 January 1961 she went to Mexico to obtain her overdue divorce from Arthur Miller. For his part, he relinquished responsibility for her with a mixture of relief and foreboding. But Marilyn had never been able to be alone. She needed a lover just to neutralise her self-loathing and she could never feel like a desirable human being without seeing herself reflected in some man's eyes. So, even before the ink was dry, she was seeing somebody else.

He was John F. Kennedy, the charismatic and newly-elected President of the United States. Their passionate but intermittent affair was pursued throughout the year at a series of secret meetings in Washington and Los Angeles hotel rooms. Almost forty years later it is hard to imagine how this relationship between the two most famous Americans of their time, both married and both constantly before the cameras, could have remained undetected by the press corps, but it has to be remembered that in those distant days American reporters who were later to pursue Nixon and Clinton so assiduously had taken a strange vow of silence. Kennedy's proclivities, which often included sex with several women a day, were well known to the White House press corps since his early campaigns for Senator in Massachusetts, but they were ignored by reporters who had become the Kennedy bandwagon as surely as the President's brothers and parents were. Occasionally, those reporters who had been particularly friendly in print to the Kennedys were rewarded by being invited to share the bounty.

It was against this background of casual sex, casually exchanged, that Marilyn (who needed to believe that she was loved and in love with all her men) was introduced to Kennedy by Peter Lawford, the English actor who was his brother-in-law and procurer-in-chief. For Jack Kennedy, Marilyn was just another prize; another of the spoils of victory. For Marilyn, who never took any of her affairs lightly, he was yet another disaster. Three times that year she was taken into clinics to have her stomach pumped and on the worst occasion of all, she was committed by a well-meaning doctor to the psychiatric ward of the Payne Whitney clinic in Los Angeles, where she found herself quite literally locked for days in a padded cell until her still-loving second husband, Joe DiMaggio, managed to extricate her by promising to take responsibility for her.

His promise was hard to keep. Marilyn, while still seeing the President, who was already tiring of her emotional demands and realizing that he could not treat America's biggest star as he did most of the other girls who passed rapidly in and out of the Oval Office, started yet another affair. This one was with Frank Sinatra, a man whose relationships with women had allegedly been sometimes transient and abusive, just the kind of man Marilyn had given up years earlier for Joe DiMaggio. It was predictable that she would once again be devastated, and she was heartbroken when a few months later Ol' Blue Eyes announced his engagement to Juliet Prowse on the very same day that Arthur Miller married Inge Morath.

Fleeing, in February 1962, to Mexico, where she somehow thought that drugs and drink and new landscapes might take her mind off the fact that this year had produced nothing but romantic disaster and lousy reviews for both *Let's Make Love* and *The Misfits*, she took on yet another lover, the young Mexican scriptwriter José Bolanos. He was seen by her side when, in March 1962, Marilyn won a Golden Globe Award, which might have done her now-moribund career a bit of good had she not been so drunk on the night of the prize-giving that all sight of her had to be removed from the edited telecast. In the words of her final film, something had to give.

EIGHT

THE LAST FILM

A sex symbol becomes just a thing and I hate that — but if I'm going to be a symbol of something, I'd rather have it be sex.

Marilyn Monroe

At the beginning of 1962, both Marilyn and George Cukor, the director of *Let's Make Love*, still owed one picture each on their contracts with Twentieth Century Fox. The studio was on the verge of bankruptcy as a result of the overspend in Italy on the endless Elizabeth Taylor–Richard Burton *Cleopatra*. Indeed, so strapped were they for cash that the studio could afford only one more picture that year; they chose therefore to bring Cukor and Monroe together again on a necessarily low budget comedy, *Something's Got to Give*, itself a remake of the 1940 Cary Grant–Irene Dunne *My Favorite Wife*, all about a woman who returns from seven years on a desert island to discover that her husband has remarried.

For the remake Marilyn was offered only $100,000, while in Rome Liz Taylor was already on a million for *Cleopatra*. Marilyn's studio salary had never in fact caught up with her fame and now it was too late. At first, despite a painful operation for the removal of her gall bladder, she seemed relieved to be back at work with a starry supporting cast of Dean Martin (in a role she had wanted Sinatra to play), Cyd Charisse, Phil Silvers and Wally Cox. But very soon all the old troubles started to surface and her co-workers found themselves hanging around on a set that Marilyn graced on only twelve of the first thirty-four days of the shooting schedule.

Initially, Cukor, together with the cast and crew, rallied around the frail and fragile Cinderella-like figure that Marilyn had become. Even when shooting had to be shut down for a fortnight when she was taken to hospital in a barbiturate coma they stuck by her. But sympathy fell rapidly away when, on returning to the set on 19 May, she announced she was once again unable to work, only to turn up in New York that night on network television singing a suggestive rendition of 'Happy Birthday' to her beloved JFK at Madison Square Garden. Few people watching this telecast could have doubted that there was something very special between her and the President but he, eager now to extricate himself from the clutches of an unpredictable neurotic, sent his brother Bobby with the news that their affair was at an end. This might have worked, had it not been that Bobby Kennedy now fell as enthusiastically for Marilyn as had his brother a year earlier; and the affair with Bobby now reduced Marilyn to yet another state of quivering inactivity.

It was too much for an already beleaguered Fox, and Cukor decided reluctantly that enough was now enough. Looking at the rushes, he realized that he had virtually nothing useable from Marilyn and he had now shot every possible scene without her. As studio costs rose exponentially, with Fox also bleeding millions in Rome, it was decided that Marilyn would have to go. On 1 June, her thirty-sixth birthday, she was told that she was to be replaced by Lee Remick. At this point Dean Martin left the set in sympathy and the film was totally abandoned until the screenplay turned up two years later as *Move Over Darling* with Doris Day and James Garner.

Monroe now had barely two months to live. Although she still photographed like a dream, her nerves were shattered and her self-esteem had reached rock bottom. It was becoming clear that Robert Kennedy, the US Attorney General, a Catholic husband and father of eight children, was not in fact going to marry her, and it is a telling symptom of her inability to separate fantasy from reality at this time that she had ever thought he might.

Despite everything, the seven minutes that survive of her last film show her radiant, striking and transcendental, but even she had never been fired before and in many ways this public repudiation by her own studio was enough to turn her frequent suicide attempts from pleas for help and attention to something rather more finite. She began to withdraw further and further into the beach house she had bought on the advice of her latest psychiatrist, whom she saw every day and who suggested that the creation of a home would prove an adequate substitute for a marriage and a child. The doctor even hired a full-time companion for her in the shape of a former nurse, Mrs Eunice Murray, and together they looked at fabric samples and colour charts when Marilyn was feeling well enough. More often Marilyn took enough drugs to sleep the clock around, and friends whom she telephoned were alarmed that she almost always fell asleep during the calls.

In these last weeks most of the Svengalis who had surrounded her Trilby whenever she was working began to fall away, leaving only Mrs Murray, a few hopeful sycophants and the ever-faithful Joe DiMaggio to try and keep her from the final abyss. It wasn't enough. But there was still drama in her life. Peter Lawford and Robert Kennedy were hovering around her waking moments, trying to ensure that her occasional threats to go public with her perfectly true stories of affairs with the President and the Attorney General were not carried out. The final humiliation was when she tried to telephone Jack Kennedy to ask him to call off his hounds and was not able to reach him at the White House because the switchboard had been given instructions not to put her through. Marilyn had already made her last public appearance on 2 June at a California Angels baseball game where she threw out the first pitch. It was her birthday present from her native State.

Fox now announced that they would sue her for breach of contract, claiming at least half a million dollars, money that ironically she could never have raised because for all these years Fox had failed to pay her the going rate for a star. Nevertheless, she now sank into a kind of twilight zone, seeing almost nobody but subjecting all those who would listen to endless nocturnal rambling phone calls which were a mixture of rage, terror, self-pity and simple incoherence, probably caused by the prodigious quantities of alcohol and barbiturates she was now consuming. In her last interview, published a few days after her death by *Life* magazine, she explained her lifelong fear of the profession she had chosen:

> A struggle with shyness is in me and all actors more than anyone can imagine; an actor is not a machine no matter how much people want to say you are. Fox executives can get colds and stay home forever and just phone it in. I would like to see them playing comedy with a temperature and a virus infection. I am not an actress who appears at the studio just for the purpose of discipline. That doesn't have anything to do with art, and surely film is supposed to be an art form not just a manufacturing business.

NINE

FINAL DAYS

Please don't make me a joke — I don't mind making jokes
but I don't want to look like one. . . . There's a future, and I
can't wait to get to it.

Marilyn Monroe, 23 June 1962

The last few weeks of Marilyn's life were not just a straight drug-induced run to the grave. Some days she was able to pick herself up, and Truman Capote, lunching with her early in June, was surprised to note, 'There was a new maturity about her eyes. She wasn't so giggly anymore and she had never looked better.' Marilyn had two last public engagements, a photo session for *Vogue* and the interview with *Life*:

Nobody knows what it is like to have all that I have and yet not be loved or know happiness. All I ever wanted out of life is to be nice to people and have them be nice to me. It's a fair exchange. And I'm a

woman. I want to be loved by a man from his heart as
I would love him from mine. I've tried but it simply
hasn't happened yet.

I really resent the way the press is now saying that
I'm depressed and in a slump, as if I'm finished.
Nothing's going to sink me although it might be kind
of a relief to be finished with moviemaking. You think
you've made it. But you never have. There's always
another scene, another film, and you always have to
start all over again. . . . I want to be an artist and an
actress with integrity; I really don't care about the
money, I just want to be wonderful.

She was dead less than a week later.

Of the 300 books that have been published about
Marilyn since her death, fifty are full-length
accounts of only the last week in her life and the
multiple, conflicting, contradictory and often
downright fantastical conspiracy theories that have
grown up around her demise.

One of these claims that she was killed by the
Mafia because she knew too much about a possible
relationship with Frank Sinatra; another that the
Kennedys somehow had her killed before she could
spill the beans on the brothers' sexual antics; time
and again the CIA has been cited as a possible

murderer because her loose-cannon sexuality meant that she was altogether too directly plugged into the innermost secrets of the United States; and there are many who believe that the shadowy carers of her last weeks killed her for the contents of her jewelbox and safe. The following facts, however, are indisputable.

At about midnight on 4 August 1962, Marilyn went to her room, taking her personal telephone with her. She bade Mrs Murray goodnight and shut her door. When Marilyn's lawyer called to check he was told that Marilyn was in her bedroom but the light was still on. At about 2 a.m., Mrs Murray says she noticed that the light was still on and she became concerned. She knocked but could get no response and finally called the ambulance service to effect a forced entry. At 3.30 in the morning of 5 August, Marilyn was found dead, nude on her bed, one arm stretched out towards the telephone. The first coroner's report declared that her death was due to 'presumed suicide caused by an overdose of barbiturates'.

It is also beyond dispute that, immediately after her body was discovered, someone cleared Marilyn's bedroom of several boxes, bottles, and papers, only some of which surfaced in later years. One of these at least proved that there was more substance than suspicion in the stories of her final affair with Robert Kennedy. It was a birthday card from Jean Kennedy Smith, the President's sister, reading simply, 'How exciting that you and Bobby are now an item'. When the card appeared mysteriously at auction in 1980 Mrs Smith first claimed that it was a forgery and then that, although it was her own handwriting, she had of course been joking.

Marilyn went down like a battleship, firing on her rescuers; it must also be admitted, though, that among those rescuers were doctors and nurses anxious to keep her totally dependent upon them and therefore inclined to allow her to abuse herself with whatever substance was available on or off prescription. The most likely cause of death, on balance and with the wisdom of almost forty years' hindsight, seems to be that Marilyn did indeed swallow, quite possibly unintentionally in her already drugged state, the overdose of hoarded Nembutal barbiturates which rapidly killed her before she could once again rescue herself by calling either Mrs Murray or a friend by telephone. However, this verdict does not rule out the fact that there were a large number of people who by now wanted her out of the way for one reason or another. In that sense, her suicide was one of the most welcome and well-timed acts that Marilyn ever succeeded in carrying through.

In death, as in life, there was only one man who could be relied on in the jungle of Hollywood to do the right thing. As soon as Joe DiMaggio heard on the radio of his former wife's death, he flew to Los Angeles and took total charge of the funeral arrangements, being careful to ban from the ceremony as many as possible of the Hollywood community whom he passionately believed had caused Marilyn's early death. The funeral took place in the Westwood Memorial Park Chapel on 8 August 1962. Inside a wooden coffin, Marilyn was wearing the green Pucci dress she had bought in Mexico a few months earlier. Of the few who were allowed by Joe into the chapel, it was her old teacher, Lee Strasberg, who gave the valediction:

We knew her as a warm human being, impulsive and shy, sensitive and in fear of rejection, yet ever avid for life and reaching out for fulfilment. . . . In her own lifetime she created a myth of what a poor girl from a deprived background could obtain. For the entire world she became a symbol of the eternally feminine. For us, Marilyn was a devoted and loyal friend, a colleague constantly reaching for perfection. . . . It is difficult to accept the fact that her zest for life has been ended by this dreadful accident. I am truly sorry that the public who loved her did not have the opportunity to see her as we did in acting class, in many of the roles that foreshadowed what she would have become. Without doubt she could have been one of the really great actresses of the stage. Now all that is at an end: I hope that her death will stir sympathy and understanding for a sensitive artist and woman who brought joy and pleasure to our world.

The crowd of thousands at the cemetery gates suggested that this was the end of an era but, like that of Eva Peron, Marilyn's fame was to grow in death. John Huston never thought that she would live to a ripe old age nor that she was the kind of person who would ever find happiness:

When she died I remember thinking it was the only possible end for the poor darling. You know where she is buried? You go into this cemetery past a bank and a car dealers and there she lies right between Wilshire and Westwood with the traffic hurtling past.

Not any more. Her body has had to be moved three times, once after an attempt to steal it and twice after the bronze headstone was stolen. There are now bus tours around Los Angeles which take you not only to every one of her houses but also to her crypt. In 1993 a classified ad in the Los Angeles Times was offering for $25,000: 'Crypt next to famous blonde moviestar, died August '62, now available for cash'. Even in death, Marilyn was still earning for all kinds of strangers.

Pauline Kael, one of the greatest of all American film writers, summed up the puzzle that was Marilyn:

> This glassy-eyed goddess is not the funny bunny that the public has always wanted. Marilyn was Lolita become Medusa, and her mixture of wide-eyed wonder and cuddly drugged sexiness seemed to get to just about every male; she even turned on homosexuals, while women could never take her seriously enough to be indignant. She was funny and impulsive in a way that made everybody feel protective. . . . Her extravagantly ripe body bulging and spilling out of her clothes, she threw herself at us with all the off-colour innocence of a baby whore . . . she was Betty Grable without the core of modesty,

the star in flagrante delicto because that's where everybody thought she belonged.

But it is left to her old friend and director John Huston to voice the exasperation that was felt by all who loved her, however fleetingly:

There's been an awful lot of crap written about Monroe and there may be some exact psychiatric term for what was wrong with her but truth to tell she was just quite mad. The mother was in a madhouse and poor Marilyn was equally loony. People say Hollywood broke her heart but that is rubbish – she was observant and tough-minded and appealing but she adored all the wrong people and she was recklessly willful. . . . You couldn't get at her. She was tremendously pretentious (she'd done a lot of shit-arsed studying in New York) but she acted as if she never understood why she was funny and that was precisely what made her so funny. . . . In certain ways she was very shrewd – her real voice was very unattractive which is why she invented this appealing baby sound. . . . Her face wasn't all that pretty but it moved in a wonderful way for movies. She just behaved the way she felt at that moment – she couldn't do otherwise. One day we had a state visit from Khrushchev which was just hilarious as they kept showing him terrible bits of *Can-Can* but Marilyn just sat there looking dazed, half the time she just didn't know what was going on. She could never sustain a scene and she had no idea about continuity but like Ava Gardner she carried a kind of excitement with her . . . if she was a victim, it was only of her own friends.

And, of course, of herself.

BIBLIOGRAPHY

Baker Miracle, Bernice and Miracle, Mona Rae. *My Sister Marilyn: A Memoir of Marilyn Monroe*, London, Orion, 1994

Brown, Peter Harry and Barham, Patte B. *Marilyn: The Last Take*, London, Heinemann, 1992

Clark, Colin. *The Prince, The Showgirl and Me, The Colin Clark Diaries*, London, Harper Collins, 1995

Guiles, Fred Lawrence. *Legend: The Life and Death of Marilyn Monroe*, London, Granada, 1984

Haspiel, James. *Marilyn: The Ultimate Look at the Legend*, London, Smith Gryphon, 1991

Luijters, Guus (ed.). *Marilyn Monroe: In Her Own Words*, London, Omnibus Press, 1990

McCann, Graham. *Marilyn Monroe*, Cambridge, Polity Press (in association with Basil Blackwell, Oxford), 1988

Mailer, Norman. *Marilyn, A Biography*, London, Hodder & Stoughton, 1973

Miller, Arthur. 'With Respect for Her Agony but with Love', *Life*, 7 February (1964)

Murray, Eunice. *Marilyn: The Last Months*, New York, Pyramid, 1975

Rollyson Jr, Carl E. *Marilyn Monroe: A Life of the Actress*, London, New English Library, Hodder & Stoughton, 1986

Rosten, Norman. *Marilyn: A Very Personal Story*, London, Millington, 1980

Bibliography

Slatzer, Robert. *The Curious Death of Marilyn Monroe*, New York, Pinnacle, 1974

Smith, Milburn. *Marilyn*, New York, Barven, 1971

Spada, James and Zeno, George. *Monroe: Her Life in Pictures*, New York, Doubleday, 1982

Spoto, Donald. *Marilyn Monroe: The Biography*, London, Arrow, 1993

Steinem, Gloria. *Marilyn: Norma Jeane*, London, Vista, 1986

Summers, Anthony. *Goddess: The Secret Lives of Marilyn Monroe*, London, Gollanz, 1985

Taylor, Roger G. (ed.), *Marilyn on Marilyn*, London, Omnibus Press, 1983

Weatherby, W.J. *Conversations with Marilyn*, London, Robson Books, 1976

POCKET BIOGRAPHIES

This series looks at the lives of those who have played a significant part in our history – from musicians to explorers, from scientists to entertainers, from writers to philosophers, from politicians to monarchs throughout the world. Concise and highly readable, with black and white plates, chronology and bibliography, these books will appeal to students and general readers alike.

Available

Beethoven
Anne Pimlott Baker

Mao Zedong
Delia Davin

Scott of the Antarctic
Michael De-la-Noy

Alexander the Great
E.E. Rice

Sigmund Freud
Stephen Wilson

Rasputin
Harold Shukman

Jane Austen
Helen Lefroy

POCKET BIOGRAPHIES

Forthcoming

Marie and Pierre Curie
John Senior

Ellen Terry
Moira Shearer

David Livingstone
Christine Nicholls

Margot Fonteyn
Alistair Macauley

Winston Churchill
Robert Blake

Abraham Lincoln
H.G. Pitt

Charles Dickens
Catherine Peters

Enid Blyton
George Greenfield